Editor Louise Cassell **Art Assistant** Sophie Heath

Hank Ketcham's DENNIS ANNUAL is published by MARVEL COMICS Ltd., Arundel House, 13/15 Arundel Street, London WC2R 3DX. Hank Ketcham's DENNIS title, design, characters, stories and artwork are copyright © 1982, 1990 North America Syndicate Inc., a subsidiary of The Hearst Corporation and part of the King Features Syndicate Group. All other material is copyright © 1990 Marvel Comics Ltd. All rights reserved. No similarity between any of the names, characters, persons and/or institutions in this annual with any living or dead person or institution is intended, and any such similarity which may exist is purely co-incidental. Printed in Italy.

CONTENTS

INTRODUCING...

DENNIS!

Hi there! My name is Dennis Mitchell, in case you didn't know. Although, come to think of it, my dad says sometimes that my middle name is 'trouble'. I don't know where he got that from, 'cos it isn't on my birth certificate.

Anyway, I was thinking that it might be fun if I was to tell you a few things about myself.

suppose I should start by telling you that for some reason or other folks around here have me down as some kind of mischief-maker. I don't know where they got that idea from. I'm just a normal five-year-old. I like having fun, but sometimes I suppose I do get a bit curious and that usually gets me into a mess! That's when mom and dad get mad at me.

Talking of mom and dad, I'd better introduce you. Mom's name is Alice and my friend Joey thinks she's real pretty. I'm lucky to have a mom like mine, though. She's great, although she does make me take yukky baths more often than I'm sure is good for me! I haven't even mentioned the number of times that I have to wash my hair, my hands, my face and the number of times I have to tidy up my room, either.

My dad's name is Henry and he's real funny. He likes to fool around a lot and he tries hard to make me and mom laugh. He does get annoyed sometimes though, when I cause trouble. Usually, that's 'cos it involves cleaning the strawberry jam off the wall, getting the peanut butter out of the carpet, or trying to wash the honey out of Ruff's fur.

Ruff's my dog, by the way. He's the best dog I know, and real fun to play with, which is just as well as I haven't got any brothers or sisters. Sometimes I think mom and dad only ever get mad at me 'cos I'm the only one to get mad at!

The other thing that seems to get me into trouble is my interest in Mr Wilson's garden. George Wilson is our neighbour, by the way, and boy can he get grouchy. He's even worse than my dad when I'm playing my drum, or when I wake him up to ask him a really important question. I guess you can't really blame him though, I do tend to get under his feet rather a lot. I know he likes me really, especially when I leave him in peace!

That just leaves my friends to tell you about. Joey is my best friend. He likes playing the same games and stuff as me, but he doesn't seem to get into as much trouble as me for some reason.

My other friend is Margaret, although I don't think 'friend' is the right word. She's a bossy sissy girl who likes ballet dancing. Yeuch! I think she's got a crush on me, too. Double yeuch! Ruff is friends with her cat Hotdog though, so she can't be all that bad.

Mr Wilson's wife Martha is really nice, I don't know how she puts up with him. He probably doesn't like her picking flowers in his garden either. At least Mrs Wilson likes me, anyway. She always gives me cookies when I go round to their house, which is more often than I think Mr Wilson likes.

Anyway, according to mom and dad it's past my bedtime, so I'd better go now. Huh! Grown-ups!

STAN LEE PRESENTS:

PLEAS!

GOLLY!

'SCUSE ME, MRS. WILSON... THIS IS A 'MERGENCY!

WHAT ON EARTH...?

LOOK AT THAT SMOKE! GOOD THING I CAME ALONG!

BUT, DENNIS! THAT'S JUST MR. WILSON...

... SMOKING HIS PIPE...!

WHAT TH...?!

9

MARTHA! WHAT'S GOTTEN INTO YOU?

DENNIS! I MIGHT HAVE KNOWN!

SORRY... I THOUGHT I WAS PUTTIN' OUT A *FIRE!*

WELL... *WAS* IT A FIRE?

NO... IT WAS ONLY MR. WILSON SMOKIN' HIS PIPE!

I'VE ALMOST MADE THE SAME MISTAKE HERE!

YA HAVE?

WE'RE NOT GONNA TURN THE HOSE ON DAD, ARE WE?

OF COURSE NOT. BUT I WISH THERE WAS *SOME* WAY WE COULD GET HIM TO STOP SMOKING!

WE COULD THROW OUT ALL HIS PIPES WHILE HE'S AT THE OFFICE!

WE COULDN'T DO THAT... HE'D BE FURIOUS!

13

PULLING STRINGS!

E veryone knows what a mischievous little boy Dennis is and how much trouble he gets into in his many adventures. If you've ever had any ideas about some good pranks to get up to, but never dared, here's your chance to let Dennis live out your dreams by making your very own Dennis Puppet!

MAKE A DENNIS PUPPET!

You will need:
A sheet of thin card
Scissors ✿
Tracing paper
Colouring crayons
Four paper clips
Cotton or string

Instructions:
1. Stick these pages onto the thin card. Cut around Dennis's arms and legs carefully. If you don't want to cut up these pages, trace Dennis and his arms and legs carefully onto the thin card, go around the outlines in black and colour in. Then continue as instructed.
2. Make holes in the card and join the arms and legs to the body, at the points marked, with the paper clips.
3. Thread a short length of cotton or string between two small holes in the arms and tie as shown, but not too tightly. Do the same with the legs.
4. Tie a length of cotton to the centre of these shorter pieces as shown.
5. Gently pull the long length of cotton and watch Dennis move!

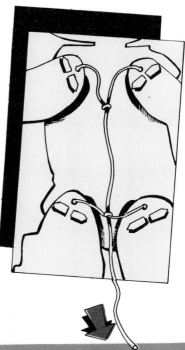

If you like, attach a piece of string to the top of Dennis' head with sticky tape and tie this to a small stick. Dennis will *really* be ready to have some fun!

✿IMPORTANT: Ask an adult to help you

The Fastest Kid in the World!

It was just a perfect day. From the moment he woke up, Dennis knew that the day was going to be perfect. *Just* fine and perfect. He could tell it from the way the sunlight was flooding into his bedroom through the crack in the curtains. He could tell it from the glorious blue sky he saw when he pulled those curtains wide. He could tell it from the way Ruff licked his face to say hello.

"Today, Ruff!" Dennis told his doggy friend as he got dressed. "Today's perfect. It's gonna be today." Dennis pulled on his dungarees and noticed that even they seem redder than usual. That clinched it. It was most definitely a sure-fire, one hundred and one per cent perfect day.

Dennis couldn't eat his cereal fast enough. "Dennis!" warned his Mom. "It isn't a schoolday! What's the hurry? Don't speak with your mouth full."

Dennis wondered which instruction he should obey first, and decided to chew rather than reply. Grown-ups! Sometimes you couldn't figure them.

As he raced out of the door with Ruff at his heels, the spoon still spinning in the empty bowl behind him, Mrs Mitchell shook her head in confusion. "Kids!" she murmured. "Sometimes you can't figure them."

Out in the backyard, Dennis and his dog leapt over the lawnmower his Dad was trundling slowly along, and disappeared towards the old shed. "What's the rush, sport?" called his Dad. "No time to stop, Dad!" Dennis called over his shoulder, "Today's a perfect day and I don't want to waste a second of it!"

Dennis slammed the shed door behind himself and his faithful friend and walked importantly over to the large thing that lay hidden under a tarpaulin in the corner. He drew back the sheet and looked in admiration at the Dennis Mitchell Racing Car Special. It was made of soap boxes and old pram wheels and it was painted bright red, even redder than Dennis' dungarees, and that sure was red.

It had taken Dennis two weeks to make, one week for the paint to dry and another to wait for the perfect conditions in which to test it. Today was that day. Today was a perfect day. Today he would take the shiny, powerful Dennis Mitchell Racing Car Special out of its garage and give it a real try out down his street. Margaret would be green with envy when she saw it.

The Special had lots of bonus features. The four baby-buggy wheels made sure it would grip the road well. A long loop of string stapled to a board attached to the front wheels meant a tug to the left or a tug to the right would send the buggy wherever Dennis wanted.

The driver sat in the cosy comfort of a plywood crate lined with the cushion from Margaret's piano stool. It was a really neat colour. On top of every thing else, the slope of the driveway at number forty-nine would mean it could race along at speeds of . . . oh, five or *six* miles per hour!

Dennis pulled the Special up the

M. KAZYBRID

slope of the driveway at number forty-nine, turned it round, put on his Rick Racer Space Hero Helmet and climbed aboard. Ruff sat on the slope next to the Special and eyed his master with concern.

Dennis lowered his visor and began to rock the cart back and forward. It started to roll. "Ruff," said Dennis, "this is going to be *perfect!*"

Then he was off! At first the Special bumped along at a walking pace, but as the slope went on, it picked up speed. The wheels were racing and the world was flashing by on either side. Ruff belted alongside and Dennis yelled in delight. This *was* perfect!

Dennis was no longer sure how fast he was going when he yanked in the string and shot round the corner at the foot of

the driveway. He charged off down the street. Ruff, hard on his heels, took the corner too fast and disappeared into the hedge at number forty-six. Dennis rattled down the pavement, a red blur. He'd never been so fast in his life, except in his Dad's car and that didn't really count. In fact he was sure he was going even faster than that, maybe two or three hundred miles per hour. He jinked round the post box, flew past the leaning gatepost at twenty-two, and leapt the kerb at the corner, whizzing like a bullet.

"Wowee!" he cried as he sped faster and faster down the road.

Time seemed to stand still as he shot through the air like a crimson dart, in the perfect sunlight. He must be going faster than anyone in the whole world! What a perfect day!

Then there was the bush. All of a sudden, without warning, the bush had got out onto the track and had planted itself firmly in the middle lane. Dennis tried to swerve, but one of the crucial staples came out of the wood in the front fork and

he was left helpless in the driving seat of the racing speed machine, with a piece of string in his hands.

He had time to say, "Darn."

The Special took off as it went through the bush, and there was an explosion of leaves. Four feet off the ground, test-pilot Mitchell and his formula one Go-Kart took down his Mom's washing line and trailed the sheets behind him like a victory flag. Then the Special touched the ground again, digging softly into the soft earth of Mr Wilson's geranium bed. There was a second explosion as the geraniums broke the fall and slowed the kart by the time it had ploughed to the far end of the bed. Then there was silence, except for the spinning of one wheel and Dennis sneezing geranium petals.

Dennis knew there would be a few more explosions when Mr Wilson and his Mom came out, but they didn't seem to matter much. He'd done it and it had been perfect. He'd become the fastest kid in the world and that was what was important. Today wouldn't get forgotten in a hurry.

It was just a perfect day.

Dan Abnett

A Gift for GEORGE

GET OUTTA HERE! BEAT IT! STAY IN YOUR OWN YARD!

WE WERE JUST PICKIN' FLOWERS FOR MRS. WILSON.

I'LL PICK MY OWN FLOWERS! NOW, **BEAT** IT!

GEORGE! PLEASE!

MY GOODNESS! MR. WILSON IS GOING TO HAVE A NERVOUS BREAKDOWN!

FAR AS I CAN SEE, HE HAS ONE EVERY DAY!

YEAH!

HE'S SURE NO **FUN** WHEN HE'S GROUCHY.

I WONDER IF THERE'S SOME WAY WE COULD MAKE HIM **HAPPY?**

24

27

MARTHA! HELP ME!

THESE KIDS ARE DRIVING ME CRAZY!

WHY, THEY HAVEN'T DONE ANYTHIN' NOR HAVE THEY UTTERED A WORD!

THAT'S HOW THEY'RE DRIVING ME CRAZY!

HONESTLY, MRS. WILSON, WE WERE JUST TRYING TO GIVE HIM WHAT HE ALWAYS WANTED...

YEAH, WHAT I TOLD YA-- PEACE AN' QUIET!

HEAR THAT GEORGE

THEIR IDEA OF PEACE AND QUIET IS MORE THAN I CAN STAND!

WELL, WE TRIED!

OF COURSE YOU DID, CHILDREN! NOW, LET'S HAVE SOME COOKIES AND...

YOU'RE NOT GOING TO FEED THEM, TOO?

29

THE BIG SCOOP!

Dennis and some of his friends think it's time for tea and that means ice cream to them! The race is on to see who can get to the ice cream first. This game can be played by two to six players. All you need are some counters (buttons or little plastic figures will do) and some dice. You roll the dice and move as many spaces as indicated and follow the instructions along the way. The first person to score the exact number to land on the finishing spot wins! It's also fun if you have some ice cream handy as a prize, although even if you win, make sure you share your good fortune with your friends! Good luck!

START..

1.

15.

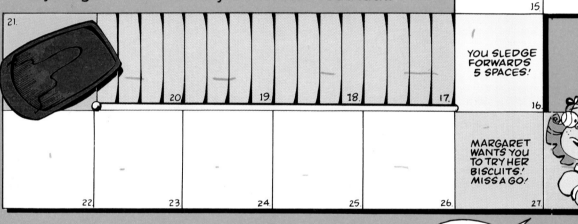

YOU SLEDGE FORWARDS 5 SPACES!

16.

MARGARET WANTS YOU TO TRY HER BISCUITS! MISS A GO!

17. 18. 19. 20. 21.

22. 23. 24. 25. 26. 27.

THEY'RE CHOCOLATE CHIP...YOUR FAVOURITE!

BREAK MUM'S BEST VASE! MISS 2 TURNS!

YOU'VE SLID ON THE RUG MOVE FORWARD 2 SPACES.

45. 44. 43. 42. 41. 40. 39.

KRAK!

BOING

46.

YOU'VE KNOCKED OVER EVERY-THING IN THE BROOM CUPBOARD! TAKE 2 TURNS TO TIDY UP!

BOUNCE OFF DAD'S CHAIR! GO 2 SPACES FORWARD.

47. 48. 49. 50. 51. 52.

GO to your ROOM!

M. KAZYBRID

M. KAZYBRID

His Mom's words were quite clear: "Dennis! Get to your room and stay there until I tell you otherwise! Maybe out of the way up there you won't be able to cause any more chaos!"

Dennis thought about arguing the point with his Mom but decided better of it. It had been a pretty big mess that he'd made with the pistachio ice cream, though it had been an important experiment. Dennis really believed he'd been helping kids all over the world by discovering how much ice cream you could eat in 30 seconds without using a spoon. He'd thought five-and-a-half jumbo scoops was pretty good going!

"What do you think you were doing, Dennis?" asked Mrs Mitchell as she shooed him upstairs to his room.

"I was finding out something really important!" replied Dennis, wiping the green ice cream off his nose and chin.

"Well now it's time for some important staying-in-your-room with nothing to fool around with," said his Mom. "You always get into trouble when there are things around to distract you. Ruff and Joey are always leading you astray. Maybe just for once you'll be at a loss for things to break, ruin or run riot with if you're shut in your room. When you have learned your lesson, I just might let you out to play in the backyard after dinner."

Mrs Mitchell closed the door and Dennis was left alone in the room. It was dim, as the curtains were shut, and only a little bit of sunlight shone through. There was nothing to do but sit in the dark and wait for Mom to set him free again. He could do nothing but sit and wait . . . there was no one to play with, or talk to or think up great ideas with. Mom had been right: this was punishment indeed.

. . . in the darkness and gloom where only a few beams of sunlight ever shone through, chief diver Dennis Mitchell circled the wreck for one final time. The powerful lamp bolted onto his heavy helmet picked out the shape of the cargo ship that lay, broken and wrecked, on the seabed. There was only one way in, through the narrow split in the busted hull, one way into the hold where, legend said, the cargo

of gold bars still lay. Diver Dennis, fearless of the sharks that circled above, crawled into the dark hole in the side of the ship . . .

Dennis peeked out from under the bed and took the lampshade off his head. It was cool and dark down here on the floor. He pulled his sweater round him and crawled back under the bed.

. . . the arctic wind howled round the edge of the ice cavern and explorer Dennis Mitchell shrank deeper into the little cave in the dark for shelter. The storm had come from nowhere and explorer Dennis knew it would be tough to last it out. Then he heard the growling outside the cave. Could it be a massive polar bear, also loking for shelter from the cruel wind? Explorer Dennis would have to wait and see . . .

Dennis climbed out from under the bed and listened to the hum of his Mom's vacuum cleaner as she cleaned the landing. Dennis clambered up and perched on the headboard.

. . . the roar of the helicopter's blades was loud in his ears as fearless rescue expert Dennis Mitchell hung from the helicopter's hatchway and looked down at the stormy mountain range below. Down there somewhere were the lost climbers and as soon as rescuer Dennis found them with his powerful searchlight, he'd be swinging down on the cable through the storm to save them. Any minute now . . .

Dennis switched off his torch and put it on the bedside table before climbing down onto the mattress again. The mattress was springy and soft and Dennis bounced on it lightly.

. . . the amazing Dennis-O, super trampoline acrobat, drew the crowds in from miles around when he performed in the big top of Mitchell and Wilson's Three Ring Circus. No one could bounce so high, or perform such incredible twists and flicks in mid-air. No one took more risks, no one was more daring or courageous. The audience cheered and applauded and hooted. Dennis-O! Dennis-O! . . .

Mrs Mitchell poked her head round the bedroom door. "Dennis?" she called. "You weren't bouncing on the bed were you?"

"No, Mom. Not really," replied the grounded acrobat.

"Well, make sure you don't. The whole point of shutting you in this room was that you wouldn't get yourself into any trouble. I don't want you busting the bedsprings or untucking all the covers."

The door closed and Dennis slumped on the bed. Mom could sure be tough sometimes. She could give him a real hard time.

. . . the chuck wagon was charging along almost uncontrollably as the two horses pulling it panicked and bolted out of the way of the massive stampede ahead of the wagon train. Wagon master Deadeye Dennis Mitchell, heaved on the reins but it was no good. He'd have to leap out onto the backs of the terrified animals and rein them in that way. Only then could he drive his wagon out of the danger. Dennis crouched and sprang . . .

Dennis landed on the bedroom chair, which wobbled under him. He tried to maintain his balance, but it was no good. Dennis and his horse-chair went flying with a crash, sending a pile of folded

35

washing up in a flurry and spilling a box of crayons.

. . . *Deadeye Dennis crashed into the dust. The horses had stumbled and the wagon had gone over. Now they lay, stunned and dusty, in the path of the oncoming stampede. Dennis struggled to rise. 'Are you all right?' asked his Mom . . .*

"Sure, Mom," replied Dennis, picking himself up. "And I wasn't doing anything. Honest."

Mrs Mitchell shook her head. "Outside, you," she said.

"What? Outside?" asked Dennis. "What do you mean? I haven't gotta weed the garden or clean the car or take the garbage out have I? What punishment are you going to give me now?"

"No punishment," laughed Mrs Mitchell. "You're going outside to play. I just realised that it doesn't matter where you are or how few distractions you have, you'll always cause trouble. Your imagination is too lively. That's just the way you are. Now scoot!"

But Dennis was already on his way.

Dan Abnett

ALL ABOUT DENNIS ...

Dennis might be your favourite comic character, but how well do you really know your mischievous little friend? Here are some simple questions to find out just how much you know about Dennis ...

1. What is Dennis' surname?
2. What are the names of Dennis' mother and father?
3. Does Dennis have any brothers or sisters?
4. What are the names of Dennis' two friends shown here?
5. What are the names of Dennis' grouchy neighbours shown in the picture?
6. What is the name of Dennis' dog shown in the picture?
7. What does Dennis think about having a bath? Does he love it or hate it?
8. What's the best way that Dennis manages to annoy his grumpy neighbours?
9. What is the name of Dennis' friend's cat as shown in the picture?
10. How old is Dennis?

If you've managed to answer all ten questions, then you're a real Dennis fan. If not, then its back to the beginning of the annual for you! Read carefully and you'll find all the answers you need.

Answers: 1. Mitchell **2.** Alice and Henry **3.** No **4.** Margaret and Joey **5.** Mr and Mrs Wilson **6.** Ruff **7.** Hate it **8.** Picking their flowers **9.** Hotdog **10.** 5.

SPOT THE DIFFERENCE!

These two pictures of Dennis getting up to his usual tricks look just the same, but if you look carefully you'll see 10 differences. See if you can circle them all and then colour in the pictures.

THE SQUEEZE PLAY

YOU HAVE TO **EARN** YOUR MONEY! WHY, WHEN **I** WAS LITTLE, I RETURNED BOTTLES FOR THE DEPOSIT!

BUT MOST STUFF COMES IN **CANS** NOW!

AND I SHOVELLED SNOW...THEY GAVE ME 10¢ FOR A WHOLE DRIVEWAY!

IT'S **SUMMERTIME** NOW!

OKAY...IN THE SUMMER I MADE AND SOLD **LEMONADE**!

YEAH! **THAT'S** WHAT WE CAN DO, DAD!

WE?

1¢ a glass

41

WHERE DID THE JUICE GO?

LET ME GUESS.

NOW LET'S DO THIS *RIGHT!*

I'LL DO THE SQUEEZING... *YOU* GET THE SUGAR!

NOW YOU'RE *TALKIN'!*

OH-OH! THE SUGAR BOWL'S EMPTY!

WELL, WHERE DOES MOTHER KEEP HER SUPPLY?

UP THERE, I THINK!

RRRIINNNG

ENRY, I FORGOT TO EFROST THE MEAT FOR UPPER. WOULD YOU...

BE *CAREFUL* DENNIS!

DENNIS! DENNIS!

43

45

46

47

KEEP COOL!

If you're always getting into hot water like Dennis, when he gets up to his tricks, here's a great way to cool down with Dennis' favourite Lemonade recipe.

Makes 3.7 litres/6½ pints.
Ingredients
350g/12oz Sugar
15ml (1 tbsp) Finely grated lemon rind
350ml/12 fl oz Hot water
350ml/12 fl oz Lemon juice

To serve:
Ice cubes
Soda water or water
Lemon syrup

What you need to do:
1. Put sugar and lemon rind into a *large* (at least 2 pint capacity) screw top jar and add the water.
2. Screw the top on and shake well until all the sugar has dissolved. Add lemon juice. Chill well.
3. Put ice into glasses. Stir in 1 part lemon syrup to 3 parts soda water or water and your refreshing drink is ready!

53

56

WHAT'S GOIN' **ON** HERE?

NOTHING, DEAR...YOU JUST HAD A BAD DREAM.

OH! PHEW! I GUESS IT WAS MY OWN FAULT FOR TAKIN' A NAP.

YOUR FAULT?

YEAH...NAPS ARE TOO **SPOOKY**! THAT'S WHY I NEVER TAKE 'EM.

WHAT **YOU** NEED IS SOME **FRESH AIR**!

GET OUT OF THOSE FLOWERS, DENNIS! BEAT IT!

GOOD OL' GROUCHY MR. WILSON!

NOW, I **KNOW** I WAS DREAMIN'!

WHAT **ELSE** IS GOING ON HERE?
BESIDES DENNIS' WILD NIGHTMARE, DID YOU NOTICE ANY OTHER STRANGE THINGS IN THIS STORY? LIKE THE SNOWMAN IN THE FLOWERBED...THE SQUARE WHEELS ON MARGARET'S DOLL CARRIAGE?
SEE HOW MANY ODDITIES YOU CAN FIND

JUST AMAZING!

Dennis is off on another big adventure. He's about to try and get from one side of this maze to the other, but he might need your help. Which way would you go?

DREAM DOG and NAP CAT

SO THEN I WOKE UP, AN' FOUND T IT WAS ALL A **BAD DREAM!**

LOOK! WHAT'S WRONG WITH RUFF?

WHY, HE'S HAVING A DREAM, TOO!

YIP! ERF!

HE'S DREAMING HE'S RUNNING! MAYBE HE'S CHASING A RABBIT!

OR SOMETHIN'S CHASIN' **HIM!**